PHOTOSYNTHESIS

Nature's Changes

CHANGING SUNLIGHT INTO FOOD

Bobbie Kalman

Crabtree Publishing Company

www.crabtreebooks.com

Created by Bobbie Kalman

For my friend Marnie, who has returned to the Light.
You will always be a part of me. Dance on with God!

Author and Editor-in-Chief
Bobbie Kalman

Editors
Molly Aloian
Kelley MacAulay
Kathryn Smithyman

Research
Niki Walker

Design
Margaret Amy Reiach
Samantha Crabtree (cover)
Robert MacGregor (series logo)

Production coordinator
Katherine Kantor

Photo research
Crystal Foxton

Consultant
Patricia Loesche, Ph.D., Animal Behavior Program,
Department of Psychology, University of Washington

Special thanks to
Jayevan Jayson Foster, Martin Izikson, and Erika Olarte

Illustrations
Barbara Bedell: pages 4, 10, 11, 17 (zooxanthellae),
 21 (owl and mouse), 26, 30
Antoinette "Cookie" Bortolon: page 24
Katherine Kantor: pages 12 (top roots), 14 (bottom), 15, 16
Margaret Amy Reiach: series logo illustrations, pages 1, 7,
 9, 14 (top), 17 (magnifying glass), 21 (sun)
Bonna Rouse: pages 6, 8, 12 (all except top roots), 13, 21 (plants)

Photographs
Marc Crabtree: page 22 (bottom right)
Bobbie Kalman: front cover, pages 22 (bottom left), 27 (top)
Other images by Comstock, Corbis, Corel, Creatas,
 Digital Stock, Digital Vision, and Photodisc

Crabtree Publishing Company

www.crabtreebooks.com   1-800-387-7650

Cataloging-in-Publication Data
Kalman, Bobbie.
 Photosynthesis : changing sunlight into food / Bobbie Kalman.
   p. cm. -- (Nature's changes series)
 Includes index.
 ISBN-13: 978-0-7787-2274-8 (RLB)
 ISBN-10: 0-7787-2274-0 (RLB)
 ISBN-13: 978-0-7787-2308-0 (pbk.)
 ISBN-10: 0-7787-2308-9 (pbk.)
 1. Photosynthesis--Juvenile literature. I. Title.
 QK882.K295 2005
 572'.46--dc22
                                        2005001095
                                        LC

**Published in
the United States**

PMB16A
350 Fifth Ave.
Suite 3308
New York, NY
10118

**Published
in Canada**

616 Welland Ave.,
St. Catharines, Ontario
Canada
L2M 5V6

**Published in the
United Kingdom**

73 Lime Walk
Headington
Oxford
OX3 7AD
United Kingdom

**Published
in Australia**

386 Mt. Alexander Rd.,
Ascot Vale (Melbourne)
VIC 3032

Contents

The first plants

A long, long time ago, there were no
plants, no animals, and no people on
Earth. Earth was covered with rocks
and oceans. Deep in the oceans, there
were tiny blue-green living things.
Some of these living things drifted
up to the top of the oceans. Many
years later, these living things
became ocean plants.

Spreading across the land

As Earth became older, the early plants changed. They started growing on land. Plants were the first living things that lived on land. Soon there were green plants growing all over Earth. The plants made food for themselves. As the plants made food, they changed the air. By changing the air, plants allowed other living things to become part of the Earth.

What are plants?

flower

leaf

stem

roots

Plants come in all shapes and sizes, but they all have the same parts. Plants have roots, leaves, and stems. Plants can also have flowers, seeds, and fruits or nuts. Nuts are a type of fruit.

Food for life

Plants, animals, and people are living things. Living things need food to stay alive. To get food, people and animals need to eat other living things.

Plants make food

Plants do not eat other living things. They are able to use sunlight to make their own food! Using sunlight to make food is called **photosynthesis**.

6

What is photosynthesis?

The word photosynthesis is made up of two words: "photo" and "synthesis." "Photo" means "light" and "synthesis" means "putting together." Plants put sunlight together with air and water to make food. The food plants make is called **glucose**. Glucose is a type of sugar.

How plants make food

Plants need more than just sunlight to make food. They need **carbon dioxide**. Carbon dioxide is a gas that is part of air. Plants also need water to make food. Some kinds of plants live in water, but most plants take in water from the soil. Soil also contains **nutrients**. Plants need nutrients to grow and to stay healthy.

Photosynthesis at work

Plants take in carbon dioxide from the air around them.

Plants use sunlight for photosynthesis.

During photosynthesis, plants lose some water through their leaves.

*When plants make food, they let off **oxygen**. Oxygen is another gas that is a part of air.*

Plants need water for photosynthesis. Most plants get water from the soil.

water

It happens in the leaves

Photosynthesis takes place in the leaves of green plants. Leaves come in all shapes and sizes. Some leaves are wide. Other leaves are long and thin. A few kinds of leaves look just like needles. The leaves of **conifers** are shaped like needles. Conifers are trees with cones.

conifer branch

cone

Veins and holes

Look at the leaf on the right. It has veins all over it. The veins carry water to parts of the leaf in the same way your veins carry blood throughout your body. Leaves are also covered with tiny holes. These holes are too small for your eyes to see. Each hole is called a **stoma**. More than one stoma are called **stomata**. Stomata take in carbon dioxide from the air. They also let off oxygen and water. Both carbon dioxide and water are needed by plants for photosynthesis.

vein

Food factories

Leaves also contain tiny **chloroplasts**, which are like little food factories. Chloroplasts contain **chlorophyll**. Chlorophyll is a green **pigment**, or natural color. It catches the sun's energy. Photosynthesis could not happen without chlorophyll!

Chlorophyll gives a leaf its green color.

Inside a leaf

Leaves are made up of tiny **cells**. Cells are the building blocks of all living things. There are different kinds of cells. Each kind performs a different job. **Guard cells** in the epidermis open and close the stomata to let out water or keep in water. The epidermis is the outside layer of a leaf. The leaf's chloroplasts are not in the epidermis. They are in other cells inside the leaf.

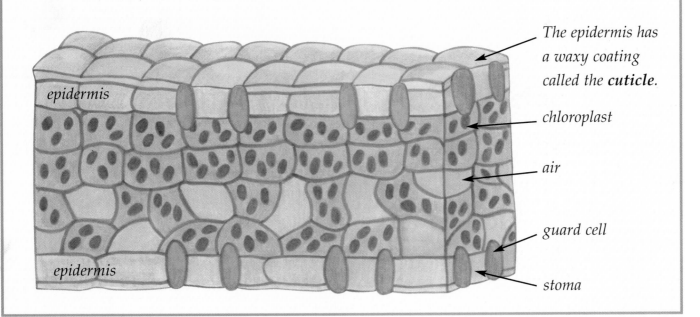

epidermis

epidermis

The epidermis has a waxy coating called the **cuticle**.

chloroplast

air

guard cell

stoma

Roots find water

Roots are the underground parts of plants. They hold plants in place in soil. They also help plants make food. The main job of roots is to take in water and nutrients from the soil. There are three kinds of roots: **taproots**, **fibrous** roots, and **runners**.

Taproots grow from one main root.

Fibrous roots spread out in all directions to find as much water as they can. Plants that grow in areas with little rain often have fibrous roots.

Runners grow from the stems of plants. The stems "run" along the ground, and roots grow down from the stems.

The jobs of stems

Plant stems are important in photosynthesis. Most stems hold up plants so their leaves can catch as much sunlight as possible. Water and nutrients travel up a plant's stem to the plant's leaves. The food made by the leaves then travels down the stem to the rest of the plant. In some plants, photosynthesis takes place in the stems.

Connecting the parts

Inside every plant there are tubes that connect all the parts of the plant. One set of tubes carries water and nutrients to the stem, leaves, and flowers. This set of tubes is called the **xylem**. Another set of tubes, called the **phloem**, carries food from the leaves to the other parts of the plant. The phloem tubes are near the outside of the stem. The **pith cells** store the extra food that the plant does not use. They are in the center of the stem.

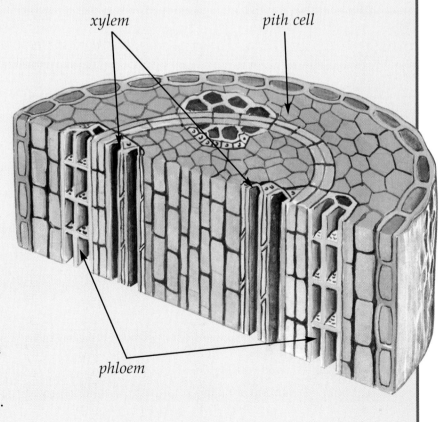

xylem

pith cell

phloem

Desert photosynthesis

The stem of a cactus contains chlorophyll. Chlorophyll takes in sunlight.

A cactus stores water in its stem. It has thick, waxy skin that helps keep the plant from losing water.

In deserts, it often does not rain for weeks or months, but plants need water for photosynthesis. Desert plants have several ways of saving water.

Stomata in the stems

The stomata of most plants are located in the leaves. In some desert plants such as cacti, however, the stomata are in the stems. In a saguaro cactus, shown left, the stomata are located in the grooves of the plant's stem. The grooves allow the cactus to expand and store water. As the cactus uses up its water, it shrinks again.

The sharp needles of a cactus keep most animals from eating the plant.

Water evaporates

Plants need to open their stomata to take in carbon dioxide. As they open their stomata, both air and water escape from the holes. In the hot desert, water **evaporates** quickly. It turns into **water vapor**.

Opening the stomata

Desert plants would lose too much water if they opened their stomata under the hot sun. To keep from losing too much water, desert plants do not open their stomata during the day. Instead, they open them at night.

Storing carbon dioxide

Desert plants take in carbon dioxide at night so the water stored in their stems will not evaporate. The plants store the carbon dioxide in their stems. Photosynthesis then takes place during the next day, when there is sunlight.

Stomata are found in the stems of cacti. They open at night to take in carbon dioxide, when they do not lose too much water.

Ocean photosynthesis

Ocean plants, called **algae**, have no trouble finding water. It is all around them! Algae are not true plants, but they perform photosynthesis in the same way land plants do. They make food using sunlight.

As algae make food, they release oxygen into ocean waters. Oceans cover most of the Earth, and they contain a lot of algae! The most important source of oxygen on Earth is algae. Algae are like the "rain forests" of the oceans.

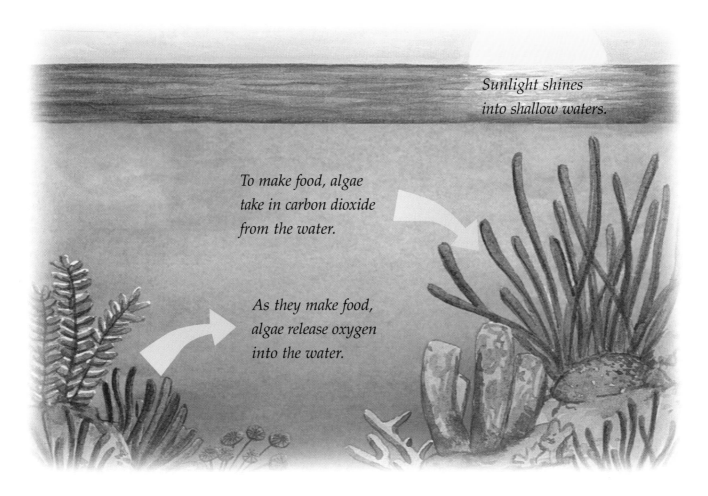

Sunlight shines into shallow waters.

To make food, algae take in carbon dioxide from the water.

As they make food, algae release oxygen into the water.

Plants inside animals

One type of algae lives inside animals called **coral polyps**. **Zooxanthellae** are tiny plants that live in the bodies of coral polyps. They have brightly colored pigments, which also make the corals colorful.

Zooxanthellae and coral polyps need each other to survive. The polyps give the zooxanthellae safe places to live and to make food. As the zooxanthellae carry out photosynthesis, they provide the polyps with food to eat and oxygen to breathe.

Coral polyps are small ocean animals that live in groups.

zooxanthellae

Energy from the sun

Everything on Earth needs **energy**, and everything is made of energy. Energy causes the wind to blow and the rain to fall. It gives living things the power to live and grow. You can't touch energy or see it, but you can't do anything without it. Even when you sleep, you are using energy. How do people and animals get energy? They get it from food!

When you eat pumpkin pie, you are getting the sun's energy that was stored in the pumpkin.

It starts with the sun

All energy starts with the sun. The energy you need comes from the sun, but you can't grab it yourself. Only green plants can! Plants are the only living things that can change the sun's energy into food.

More than they need

The glucose that plants make is the source of energy for all living things. When plants make glucose, they make more than they need. As a result, plants have extra food.

Stored energy

Plants store their extra food as energy. They store the energy in their leaves, stems, fruits, and roots. When you eat food, you also store some food energy in your body.

Energy is passed along

Some animals eat only plants to get energy. Plant-eating animals are called **herbivores**. Herbivores get the sun's energy that was stored in plants. They use some of the energy and store the rest in their bodies. Not all animals eat plants, however.

Many animals eat other animals. Animals that eat other animals are called **carnivores**.

What is a food chain?

When a carnivore eats a herbivore, it still gets some of the sun's energy, but it does not get the energy directly from plants. The carnivore gets the energy from the animal that has eaten the plants. Energy is passed from plants to animals in **food chains**. All food chains start with photosynthesis.

This egret is eating a frog that ate an insect that ate a plant that made food using sunlight. Every food chain starts with photosynthesis!

How a food chain works

A food chain is the pattern of eating and being eaten. Look at this diagram to see how a food chain works. The arrows show which way the energy flows.

Plants make food

During photosynthesis, green plants use the sun's energy to make food. They use some of the energy and store the rest. Plants are called **producers** because they **produce**, or make, food.

Herbivores eat plants

When an animal such as a mouse eats a plant, it gets some of the sun's energy that was stored in the plant. Herbivores are called **primary consumers** because they are the **primary**, or first, group of living things to **consume**, or eat, food.

Carnivore energy

When a carnivore, such as an owl, eats a mouse, energy is passed to the owl through the plant and then the mouse. The owl is a **secondary consumer**. Secondary consumers are the second group of living things that need to eat to get food energy. They eat primary consumers.

sun

plants

mouse

owl

Photosynthesis and you!

Just like the food of other living things, your food starts with photosynthesis! Most people are **omnivores**. Omnivores eat both plant and animal foods.

When you eat meat and plant foods, you are part of many food chains. The sun's energy is passed along to you through the plants and meat you eat.

Every kind of food you eat started with photosynthesis!

Breathe!!!

Not only do you get food through photosynthesis, but you also get the air you breathe. Plants take carbon dioxide from air to make food. Too much of this gas in air is harmful to humans and to many other living things.

Plants release oxygen into the air during photosynthesis. Animals and people need oxygen to breathe. Forests add huge amounts of oxygen to the air. Ocean plants add even more oxygen. Without plants, we would not have oxygen to breathe!

Plants in winter

In places that have cold winters, many plants, including trees, become **dormant**. When plants are dormant, they are not active, and they do not make food.

Sunlight and water

In winter, there are fewer hours of sunlight. The roots of plants cannot get much water because the ground is frozen.

Losing their leaves

The leaves of **deciduous trees** change color because the chlorophyll in them starts to break down. Without chlorophyll to catch sunlight, the leaves cannot make food. When the leaves die, they drop off the trees.

In spring and summer, the leaves of deciduous trees are green from chlorophyll.

In autumn, deciduous leaves lose their chlorophyll. As a result, their colors turn yellow and orange.

The red color in leaves is caused by the glucose still stored in leaves after photosynthesis has stopped.

The brown color is caused by the waste left in leaves after the chlorophyll and glucose are gone.

Test your plant IQ

Look at the pictures on this page and guess which of these living things can make food. The answers are below.

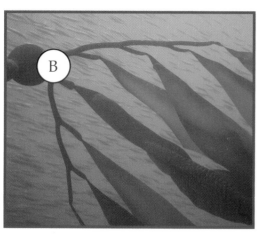

Which parts do we eat?

Plants store food energy in their roots, leaves, stems, fruits, and seeds. The pictures on this page show different parts of plants that people eat. Guess which plant parts they are. Match the numbers with the correct plant parts. The answers are in the box below.

The plant parts are:

stems   flowers   roots
leaves   seeds   fruits

Answers:

6. Peas are seeds.
5. Carrots are roots.
4. Grapes are fruits.
3. Celery stalks are stems.
2. Cauliflower is a flower.
1. Lettuce is made up of leaves.

27

Amazing plants!

Even dead leaves help feed living things. They are eaten by worms, mushrooms, and bacteria. The energy that is left in the leaves is put back into the soil and helps new plants grow.

This tiny bobcat lives in the trunk of a dead tree.

You already know that plants make all the food and oxygen on Earth, but plants are amazing in other ways, too!

From the soil to the sky

Plants help **circulate** water. The roots of plants search for water in the ground to use for photosynthesis. While plants make food, they give off water vapor. The water that came from below the ground now becomes part of the water that is in the air.

Homes for many creatures

Plants provide animals with shelter. Squirrels, bobcats, and many birds live in the trunks or branches of trees. All kinds of animals, including insects, live on, in, or among plants. People also use trees and other plants to build homes and to make furniture.

Don't eat me!

Plants feed the world, but they also need to stay alive. Some plants keep animals from eating them by having sharp thorns or needles. A few kinds of plants send emergency "calls" to other plants or to insects.

Special smells

These "calls" help save the plants. Bean plants, cotton plants, and maize plants are all able to send out certain smells when too many insects are eating them. The smells bring other insects to eat the insects that are eating the plants.

Giraffe attack!

Giraffes live in Africa. They eat acacia trees. Acacia trees make a bitter-tasting chemical called **tannin**. Too much tannin is poisonous to giraffes. When giraffes munch on the branches of an acacia tree, they do not have long to eat! Within 30 minutes, the branches send out an emergency call to the rest of the tree to make more tannin. Not only does the tree get the message, but nearby acacia trees receive the message, as well. They make more tannin, too. To keep from being poisoned, giraffes need to keep moving to new areas to find enough food.

Thank you plants!

Plants bring beauty to our lives. They please all our **senses**. Our senses are sight, smell, touch, hearing, and taste.

- We love to look at plants in parks, gardens, and **meadows**.
- We enjoy smelling flowers.
- We like the feel of soft grass under our feet.
- The sound of silence in a forest makes us feel peaceful.
- We love the delicious tastes of fruits and vegetables.

A poem of thanks

Write a thank-you poem to plants. Use this poem to get some ideas.

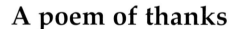

Thank you plants for the food I eat.
Thank you plants for the air I breathe.
Thank you flowers for bringing butterflies.
Thank you trees for reaching to the skies.
Thank you plants for working hard for me,
and thank you plants for doing it for free!

Everyone loves to look at—and smell—beautiful flowers!

It feels great to walk and dance barefoot on grass.

Get outdoors!

Without photosynthesis, there would be no nature. Think about it! To understand how important photosynthesis really is in your life, spend more time in nature. Get your whole family outdoors!

You are a part of nature!

You are connected to nature through the food you eat and the air you breathe. Feel that connection with all your senses!

- Go hiking in a forest. Name ten things you see.
- Stand with your back against a tree and feel the energy of the tree in its trunk. Think of five ways in which you are connected to trees.
- Listen! What do you hear? Is wind rustling through the tree's leaves? Are birds chirping?
- Close your eyes. How does the air smell?

Words to know

Note: Boldfaced words that are defined in the text may not appear in the glossary.

algae Plantlike living things in water that use the sun's energy to make food

cell The most basic part of every living thing; most plants and animals are made of millions of cells

chloroplasts Tiny structures in the cells of green plants that contain the plant's chlorophyll

circulate To move around from one place to another

coral polyps Ocean animals that live in groups and form corals

deciduous tree A tree that loses its leaves in autumn

meadow A large, open grassy area

nutrients Substances that help living things grow and stay healthy

omnivore A living thing that eats both plant and animal foods

water vapor Droplets of water in air

Index

1 2 3 4 5 6 7 8 9 0   Printed in the U.S.A.   4 3 2 1 0 9 8 7 6 5